EXPLORING COUNTRIES

# BRAZIL

Tracy Vonder Brink

## TABLE OF CONTENTS



A Crabtree Seedlings Book

Crabtree Publishing

crabtreebooks.com

# School-to-Home Support for Caregivers and Teachers

This book helps children grow by letting them practice reading. Here are a few guiding questions to help the reader with building his or her comprehension skills. Possible answers appear here in red.

## Before Reading:

- What do I think this book is about?
    - *I think this book is about Brazil.*
    - *I think this book is about places to visit in Brazil.*

- What do I want to learn about this topic?
    - *I want to learn where Brazil is.*
    - *I want to learn about some of Brazil's cities.*

## During Reading:

- I wonder why...
    - *I wonder why Brasília is shaped like an airplane.*
    - *I wonder why so many fish live in the Amazon River.*

- What have I learned so far?
    - *I have learned that Brazil is in South America.*
    - *I have learned that there is a famous statue in Rio de Janeiro.*

## After Reading:

- What details did I learn about this topic?
    - *I have learned that Brazil has more than 2,000 beaches.*
    - *I have learned that sloths live in the rain forest in Brazil.*

- Read the book again and look for the vocabulary words.
    - *I see the word* ***capital*** *on page 4, and the word* ***coast*** *on page 6. The other glossary words are on pages 22 and 23.*

Brazil is a country.

It is in **South America**.

Brasília is the **capital** of Brazil.

From above, the city looks like an airplane or a bird.

Most people in Brazil speak Portuguese.

Brazil has a long **coast**.

The longest beach in the world is in Brazil.

The coast has more than 2,000 beaches.

Rio de Janeiro is a large city on the coast.

A famous **statue** stands above the city.

The statue is 98 feet (30 m) tall.

São Paulo is Brazil’s biggest city.

More than 12 million people live there.

São Paulo has a large market.

Shoppers buy fresh fruits, vegetables, and other foods there.

THEATRO PEDRO II

MELÃO KG
AMARELO
MELÃO
AMARELO
KG
R$
kg
3,99
extra

Brazil has many rivers.

The Amazon River is the longest.

The Amazon River is the second-longest river in the world.

More than 3,000 kinds of fish live there.

The river flows through the Amazon **rain forest**.

It is the largest rain forest in the world.

About 80,000 kinds of plants grow in the rain forest.

Tall trees stretch to the sky.

Colorful flowers bloom.

Many **unique** animals make their homes in the rain forest.

Sloths and golden lion tamarins live in the trees.

Brazil is an amazing country!

# Glossary

**capital** (KAP-i-tl): The city where the government of a country or a state is located

**coast** (kohst): The land next to the ocean or sea

**rain forest** (RAYN faw-ruhst): A dense, tropical forest that has a large amount of rainfall

**South America** (SOWTH uh-MEH-rih-kuh): One of Earth's seven continents, located below North America

**statue** (STA-choo): A figure of a person or an animal made by an artist from a hard material such as metal or stone

**unique** (yoo-NEEK): Very special and unlike anything else

# Index



# About the Author

## Tracy Vonder Brink

Tracy Vonder Brink loves to visit new places. She has never been to Brazil, but she has held a sloth. She lives in Cincinnati, Ohio, with her husband, two daughters, and two rescue dogs.

Written by: Tracy Vonder Brink
Designed by: Rhea Magaro
Series Development: James Earley
Proofreader: Melissa Boyce
Educational Consultant: Marie Lemke M.Ed.

Photographs: All images from Shutterstock

**Crabtree Publishing**

**crabtreebooks.com 800-387-7650**



Printed in the U.S.A./062024/CG20240201

**Published in Canada**
**Crabtree Publishing**
616 Welland Avenue
St. Catharines, Ontario
L2M 5V6

**Published in the United States**
**Crabtree Publishing**
347 Fifth Avenue
Suite 1402-145
New York, New York, 10016

**Library and Archives Canada Cataloguing in Publication**
Available at Library and Archives Canada

**Library of Congress Cataloging-in-Publication Data**
Available at the Library of Congress

Hardcover: 978-1-0398-4477-3
Paperback: 978-1-0398-4558-9
Ebook (pdf): 978-1-0398-4630-2
Epub: 978-1-0398-4700-2
Read-Along: 978-1-0398-4770-5
Audio: 978-1-0398-4840-5